BIOGRAPHIES

MARIAN ANDERSON

by Laura K. Murray

Pebble Explore is published by Pebble, an imprint of Capstone.
1710 Roe Crest Drive
North Mankato, Minnesota 56003
www.capstonepub.com

Copyright © 2022 by Capstone.
All rights reserved. No part of this publication may be reproduced in whole or in part, or stored in a retrieval system, or transmitted in any form or by any means, electronic, mechanical, photocopying, recording, or otherwise, without written permission of the publisher.

Library of Congress Cataloging-in-Publication Data
Names: Murray, Lisa K., author.
Title: Marian Anderson / by Lisa K. Murray.
Description: North Mankato : Pebble, 2021. | Series: Biographies | Includes bibliographical references and index. | Audience: Ages 5-8 | Audience: Grades 2-3 |
Summary: "How much do you know about Marian Anderson? Find out the facts you need to know about this singer. You'll learn about the early life, challenges, and major accomplishments of this important American"-- Provided by publisher. Identifiers: LCCN 2021004165 (print) | LCCN 2021004166 (ebook) | ISBN 9781977132086 (hardcover) | ISBN 9781977154620 (pdf) | ISBN 9781977156280 (kindle edition)
Subjects: LCSH: Anderson, Marian, 1897-1993--Juvenile literature. | Contraltos--United States--Biography--Juvenile literature. | African American singers--Biography--Juvenile literature. Classification: LCC ML3930.A5 M87 2021 (print) | LCC ML3930.A5 (ebook) | DDC 782.1092 [B]--dc23 LC record available at https://lccn.loc.gov/2021004165 LC ebook record available at https://lccn.loc.gov/2021004166

Image Credits
Associated Press: 22, Douglas Healey, 24; Franklin D. Roosevelt Library and Museum: 16; Getty Images: Archive Photos, 21, Bettmann, cover, 1, 10, 19, 23, Gado/Afro American Newspapers, 15; Library of Congress: 5, 7, 17, 29; The New York Public Library: 9; Newscom: Everett Collection, 18, ZUMA Press/Mario Ruiz, 27; Shutterstock: Alex Landa (geometric background), cover, back cover, 2, 29, catwalker, 25, DW labs Incorporated, 13

Editorial Credits
Editor: Erika L. Shores; Designer: Elyse White; Media Researcher: Svetlana Zhurkin; Production Specialist: Spencer Rosio

All internet sites appearing in back matter were available and accurate when this book was sent to press.

Printed and bound in China. 5241

Table of Contents

Who Was Marian Anderson? 4
Growing Up 6
Singing Out 14
A Leader for All 18
Remembering Marian 24

Important Dates 28
Fast Facts 29
Glossary 30
Read More 31
Internet Sites 31
Index 32

Words in **bold** are in the glossary.

Who Was Marian Anderson?

Marian Anderson was a famous American singer. She performed in the 1920s through 1960s. People said she had the most beautiful voice they had ever heard.

Marian made history for more than her voice. During Marian's life, the United States went through many changes. All Americans were supposed to be free and equal. But Marian and other Black Americans were treated unfairly because of their skin color. Marian changed music and American history forever.

Marian Anderson in 1940

Growing Up

Marian was born February 27, 1897, in Philadelphia, Pennsylvania. She had two younger sisters. Their names were Alyse and Ethel.

Marian started singing in her church choir at age 6. She could sing low and high notes. By age 8, she got small singing jobs. Her family did not have money for lessons. But Marian learned all she could from other singers. She taught herself to play piano. She took cleaning jobs to get money for a violin.

Philadelphia in the early 1900s

In 1910, Marian's father died. Marian was 12 years old. Her family moved in with her grandparents. Marian's mother took cleaning jobs. But they could not afford for Marian to go to high school.

Marian kept singing in the church choir. Her church and neighbors helped pay for music lessons. Later they helped her to go to school. In 1921, Marian finished high school at age 24.

Members of a Baptist church choir in Philadelphia in 1922

Marian wanted to go to a music school in Philadelphia. The school would not let Black Americans go there. Marian did not let that stop her from studying music. She learned from Black singers and musicians. She studied with a famous voice teacher.

Marian sang **contralto**. Her voice was rich and low. She learned to sing **opera** and many other types of music. She also loved to sing about the history of Black Americans.

In 1925, Marian won a singing contest at age 28. She got to perform with the New York Philharmonic **Orchestra**. In 1928, she sang at Carnegie Hall. It is a famous place for concerts in New York City. People were amazed at her talent.

Still, it was hard for Marian to get singing jobs. People treated her unfairly because of her skin color. Some white people did not let her stay in their hotels. They did not let her eat in their restaurants.

Carnegie Hall

Singing Out

Marian decided to go to Europe to sing and study music. In the early 1930s, Marian went on **tours** across Europe. She became famous there.

Soon people around the world knew Marian's name. Music **conductors** had never heard a voice like hers. In 1936, she was the first Black American to sing at the White House. She sang in front of U.S. President Franklin D. Roosevelt and First Lady Eleanor Roosevelt.

A poster for Marian's concert in 1931 praised her talent.

In 1939, Marian was going to give a concert in Washington, D.C. But a white women's group would not let her use their big concert hall. Many people thought it was wrong. Eleanor Roosevelt and other women quit the group in **protest**. Eleanor helped Marian find another place to sing.

First Lady Eleanor Roosevelt

Marian singing at the Lincoln Memorial

On April 9, 1939, Marian sang on the steps of the Lincoln Memorial. She was 42. More than 75,000 people stood in the crowd. They were all races and ages. Millions more listened on the radio.

A Leader for All

In 1943, Marian married Orpheus Fisher in Bethel, Connecticut. Marian became stepmother to Orpheus's son, James. Marian and her family lived on a farm in Danbury, Connecticut. They built a studio for Marian to work on her music.

Marian and her husband in 1954

Marian sang at the Met in New York City in 1955.

On January 7, 1955, Marian sang at the Metropolitan Opera in New York City. It is known as the Met. Marian was the first Black American to sing there. She was 57 years old.

During her life, Marian sang for many world leaders. In 1957, she sang for U.S. President Dwight D. Eisenhower. Four years later, she sang for President John F. Kennedy.

Marian worked to helped make life better for others. She gave concerts to help the **Civil Rights Movement**. In 1963, she sang at the March on Washington. It was in Washington, D.C. It called for the **rights** of Black Americans.

Marian sang at the March on Washington.

Marian won many awards for singing. She also won awards for her work for equal rights. In 1963, she received the Presidential Medal of Freedom. It was for all she had done in her life.

Marian receiving the Presidential Medal of Freedom

Marian at Carnegie Hall in 1988

Marian lived at her farm until the 1990s. Then she went to live with her nephew. Marian died April 8, 1993, in Portland, Oregon. She was 96. More than 2,000 people came to say goodbye at Carnegie Hall.

Remembering Marian

Today, people remember Marian's life. They listen to her music. They watch videos of her concerts.
They visit her studio in Connecticut. It is part of the Danbury Museum.

The Marian Anderson studio in Danbury, Connecticut

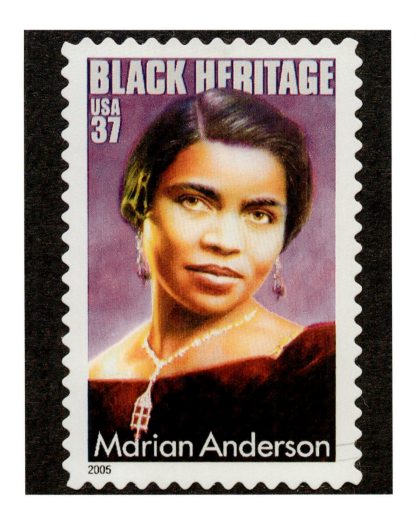

People have written books about Marian. They make art and films about her. In 2005, the U.S. made a postage stamp with her picture.

Marian Anderson was a talented singer. She helped shape American music. She also fought to make life better for others. She had hard times. She was treated unfairly. But she kept working hard.

Marian inspires many singers and artists today. She showed what is possible. She helped lift others up. She never stopped following her dreams.

Marian in 1979

Important Dates

February 27, 1897	Marian Anderson is born in Philadelphia, Pennsylvania.
1925	Marian wins a singing contest and gets to sing with the New York Philharmonic Orchestra.
1928	Marian becomes the first Black American to sing at Carnegie Hall in New York City.
1936	Marian becomes the first Black American to sing at the White House.
April 9, 1939	Marian sings on the steps of the Lincoln Memorial.
July 1943	Marian marries Orpheus Fisher in Bethel, Connecticut.
1955	Marian becomes the first Black American to sing at the Metropolitan Opera in New York City.
1963	Marian sings at the March on Washington in Washington, D.C.
1963	Marian receives the Presidential Medal of Freedom.
April 8, 1993	Marian dies at age 96 in Portland, Oregon.

Fast Facts

Name:
Marian Anderson

Role:
singer

Life dates:
February 27, 1897 to April 8, 1993

Key accomplishments:
Marian Anderson was a famous American singer. More than 75,000 people came to her 1939 concert on the steps of the Lincoln Memorial. She became the first Black American to perform in places such as the White House and the Met. She fought for the rights of Black Americans.

Glossary

Civil Rights Movement (SI-vil RYTS MOOV-muhnt)—the fight for the equal rights of Black Americans in the United States during the 1950s and 1960s

conductor (kuhn-DUHK-tuhr)—the person in charge of a choir or orchestra

contralto (kahn-TRAL-toh)—the lowest female singing voice

opera (OP-ur-uh)—a play in which the words are sung

orchestra (OR-kuh-struh)—a group of people playing classical music with different types of instruments

protest (PRO-test)—to speak out against something strongly and publicly

right (RITE)—something that everyone should be able to do or to have and that the government shouldn't be able to take away, such as the right to speak freely

tour (TOOR)—a group of shows or concerts in different cities

Read More

Haldy, Emma E. *Marian Anderson*. Ann Arbor, MI: Cherry Lake Publishing, 2017.

Rose, Lisa. *The Singer and the Scientist*. Minneapolis: Kar-Ben Publishing, 2021

Internet Sites

Marian Anderson: Musical Icon
pbs.org/wgbh/americanexperience/features/eleanor-anderson/

Marian Anderson Sings at the Lincoln Memorial
youtube.com/watch?v=XF9Quk0QhSE

Index

birth, 6, 28, 29

Carnegie Hall, 12, 23, 28

church choirs, 6, 8

Civil Rights Movement, 20

contralto, 10

death, 23, 28, 29

Europe, 14

family, 6, 8, 18, 23

high school, 8

Lincoln Memorial, 17, 28, 29

March on Washington, 20, 28

marriage, 18, 28

Metropolitan Opera, 19, 28, 29

New York Philharmonic Orchestra, 12, 28

opera, 10

Presidential Medal of Freedom, 22, 28

Roosevelt, Eleanor, 14, 16

Roosevelt, President Franklin D., 14

studio, 18, 24

tours, 14

voice, 4, 10, 14

White House, 14, 28, 29